© **Jason Kasper 2020**

All rights reserved. No part of this publication may be reproduced, stored in a retrieval system, or transmitted in any form or by any means, electronic, mechanical, photocopying, recording, or otherwise, without the prior written permission of the author.

Contents

Chapter 1..1

Introduction to Metal Detecting

Basic Theory in Metal Detecting

How does Metal Detector Work?

My First Experience with Metal Detector

How I fell in Love with Metal Detecting

Types of Metal Detector

Beat Frequency Oscillation Metal Detector (BFO)

Very Low Frequency Metal Detector

Pulse Induction Metal Detector

Reasons for Going Into Metal Detecting

Why go Metal Detecting?

Tips for Metal Detecting

Chapter 2..**11**

Learning the Lingo of Metal Detecting

How to use Your Metal Detector to Hunt

Chapter 3..**19**

What your Detector tells You

Audio Tone

Target Indicator

Target ID Number

Search Coil

Know Your Machine

Mineralization

Metal Detector Classes

White's Metal Detector

Garret ACE 250 Metal Detector

Hunting with Your Garrett ACE 250 Metal Detector

Can Garrett Ace 250 Find Gold?

Is a Garrett ACE 250 a Good all Rounder?

Teknetics Metal Detector

Minelab Metal Detector

Frequently asked Questions

XP Metal Detector

Bounty Hunter TK4 Tracker IV

Features and Settings

Some Usually Ask Questions

Chapter 4……………………………………………………….37

Relic Metal Detector

Coins Shooting Metal Detector

Underwater Metal Detector

Gold Metal Detector

Metal Detectors for Kids

Multipurpose Metal Detector

Chapter 5...47

How to Clean Up Your Metal Detector Finds

How to clean Your Found Coins

Jewelry Cleaning

How to Clean Up Your Gold

How to clean Iron Relics Using Electrolysis

Steps You can Take to clean up lost Relics

How to preserve Your Iron Relics

Rules of Metal Detecting

Getting Permission for Metal Detecting

Chapter 6...58

How can You Find Buried Treasure?

Where should I start metal detecting?

Can You Make Money from Metal Detecting?

What is the Best Metal Detector in the Market?

Metal Detector Accessories

How to recover a Target

How to research for Treasure

Chapter 7……………………………………………..71

Detecting for Treasures in River and Stream

How to identify Your Metal Detector Finds?

How You Can Identify Coins?

How to Identify Relics

How to Identify Jewelry

How to sell Your Finds?

Joining a Metal Detecting Club

Chapter 1

Introduction to Metal Detecting

Metal detecting is the processing of discovering precious and valuable metals using a major tool called metal detector. In this book I will teach you on how to find treasures. I will also cover the equipment you need to make the hunt for metals successful, and locations. You will also learn other key skills and precautionary measures you need base on my level of experience.

Basic Theory in Metal Detecting

Metal detector is an electronic instrument used in detecting the presence of metal in a place or a tool used to indicate the availability of metal buried for a long time. Metal detectors are very important because they are used in finding hidden treasures (gold, silver, coins, and relics) which was buried underground during wars and in other occasions. We can find different kinds of metal in oceans, forest, beach, parks, old building, abandon cities where wars took place before. By using metal detector which often consist of a handheld unit with a sensor probe which can be swept over the ground, if the sensor comes in contact with any pieces of metal, it will give beeps. The closer the metal the higher the sound of the sensor (a sensor is a device, machine or a subsystem which its characteristic is to detect event or changes in it environment). Usually the device gives some indication of distance.

Metal detectors are used also in different organizations, office, courthouse, airport to detect the present of weapon in the bags of individuals and also on their body to know if there are hidden dangerous equipment before allowing any individual inside the building.

How does Metal Detector Work?

Metal detector works by transmitting electromagnetic field from the coil into the ground. Any metal object found by the electromagnetic field will be energised and they will retransmit their own electromagnetic field. The detector search coil will receive the retransmitted electromagnetic field and alert the user by producing a target response.

My First Experience with Metal Detector

My first experience using detector was on my 15th birthday which falls on Easter Sunday. I can remember vividly when my dad and mom presented a wrapped gift to me. I never knew what it was because I have never set my eyes on such package before. I was actually angry because that was not what I was expecting from them before, but when I opened the gift, I saw bounty hunter metal detector. My thinking was what am I going to do with this thing. But I had to accept it because it was coming from my forever loved parents. I appreciated them and inside my inner heart I was not that happy as I displayed physically. After the party, the next day my dad called me and ask me to bring out my gift that he would like to perform some experiments. I rush inside and got the detector.

After I handed it over to him, he opened it and brought out the manual inside. He followed the procedure on how to set it up and when I asked him what the detector was all about, he told me it is used to detect precious metals underground. Hearing this, I was so happy. He said his friends were discussing how the detector works so he decided to get it for me so that during my holiday I can be making use of it at least to keep me busy. So, hearing about precious metal detecting with the metal detector, I become interested.

How I fell in Love with Metal Detecting

Our first hunting was in the compound, I and my dad went hunting near the house and we found few metals which one of them was my mom's lost gold chain which was a little bit costly. My mom was happy to see her long lost gold necklace. We also found some irons in the ground. Both our lost house key was detected that day. I and my dad were so happy for what we found and that motivated me. In my first hunting (I hunted alone), I went near beach with my friend and I found 3 gold rings. When I sold those rings, I made some money from it. Because of that experience, since then my quest for treasure hunt increased. That is how I love hunting with metal detector because I make a little cash from it. It is also fun whenever I go with my friends. Sometimes we went to the beach or forest to look for treasure and I personally purchased some other metal detectors with the money I made from my sales and some of my friends also got theirs which also makes the hunting much fun.

Types of Metal Detector

The three-basic classification of metal detector are:
- Beat frequency oscillation metal detector (BFO)

- Very low frequency metal detector (VLF)
- Pulse induction metal detector (PI)

Beat Frequency Oscillation Metal Detector (BFO)

The beat frequency oscillation metal detector (BFO) is one of the most basic metal detection system. It has six modified analog circuit which comprises one digital circuit and many basic components. The headphone Jack of the beat frequency oscillation serve as the "**output**" with potmeter determining tune and volume while the inductor coils capacitance serves as the "**input**". Beat frequency oscillation metal detector system uses a search coil to detect a metallic object at a close range and give a visual, auditory and vibratory indication once the gold, silver or any treasure is found.

BFO is generally the simplest type of metal detecting and is a good starting point for those who are just starting the learning of how metal detecting work. The basic beat frequency oscillation metal detector hires two radio frequency oscillators which are tuned near the same frequency. The first radio frequency is called the search oscillator while the second radio frequency is called the reference oscillator.

The output of two oscillators are include into mixer which yield a signal that contains the sum and difference frequency components.

The signal is content to a low pass filter removing the harmonics once the two oscillators are tuned to the same frequency, the output will have no signal.

If any metallic object such as gold, silver disturbs the magnetic field of the search coil, the frequency of the search oscillator shifts slightly, and the detector will produce a signal in the audio frequency range. The BFO metal detector is an inexpensive metal detector and are simple to handle.

Very Low Frequency Metal Detector

Very low frequency (VLF) metal detector is the most popular detector technology in use today. You can easily find this kind of detector in the market than beat frequency oscillation metal detector. It is also known as induction balance. Very low frequency metal detector has two distinct coil which are transmitter coil and receiver coil. The coil usually operates in 5.5kHZ frequency range. The amplitude and phase detection circuits were designed to detect and distinguish between different kinds of metal. It usually detects between these three types of metal which are aluminium, copper and iron at various distances. It can detect metals that is 15cm below the ground. Transmitter coil is the outer coil loop while the inner coil loop, the receiver, contains another coil of wire. This coil wire acts as an antenna to pick up and amplify frequency coming from object that is underground. Very low frequency metal detector offers higher sensitivity at high frequency.

Pulse Induction Metal Detector

Pulse induction metal detector is a technology which offers more depth in mineralized ground. Pulse metal detectors are different from the other types of detectors. There is single coil which acts as the receiver and transmitter, and it sends bursts of current through the coil into the ground at the potential target.

Reasons for Going into Metal Detecting

These questions might be running through your mind like why do you need to go for hunting of metals? What are the benefits of the hunting? Does the hunting worth time spending? Where can you start with your hunting?

Your thinking is cool if all these questions are actually running through your mind. My first hunting was not actually that fun because I got tired for some time before I was able to discover my little treasure.

But before you go into finding of different kinds of metal of your choice like gold, relics, jewelry, silver or any treasure you can think of, you have to know exactly what you want to get or hunt for because some metal detectors go for a particular purpose. You might be a lover of gold and because of that you need to go for a metal detector that are specialize for gold finding.

Also, you might be a lover of silver and diamond. You will need to go for a metal detector which are specialize in finding these kinds of metal. You cannot have a gold metal detector and expect it to work perfectly well on detecting diamond. So, before you go into metal detecting hunting, you have to know which kind of metal you like mostly because that will also give you courage to hunt more and it will make the hunting look fun to you whenever you remember whatever you stand to gain .There are lot of hundred metal detectors in the market today and choosing which one is good for you is somehow complicated because some detectors are made for different purposes.

Sometimes, you might like to hunt for different kinds of treasures at the same time. You are really on a right track because technology has made it a reality. They have produced detectors which are multipurpose, and they performed different task on hunting metals such as gold, silver and so on. Digging up trash is part of metal detecting game, but your metal detector is there to help you out because it will ignore some trash if not all.

Why go Metal Detecting?

Some people have different opinions why they like to go for hunting for different kinds of metal. The reason why Williams goes into metal detecting may not be the same reason Ronaldo also goes to metal hunt. We have different views in going to metal detecting. One of the reasons some people go into metal detecting is because of financial gain from either selling your finds (gold/silver jewelry) or even gold nuggets. While another reason is the love of being active and in the outdoors. Believe it or not, metal detecting can be a fantastic form of exercise.

Secondly some people also go into hunting of metal because the love of coin collecting. Whether that be older colonial silver coins or more modern coins like wheat pennies.

Tips for Metal Detecting

Metal detecting is a great hobby and it can also be frustrating especially when you use your energy to dig a particular spot and at the end of the digging you found out it is a trash. It can be very annoying when you have such experience. You know the saying "practice is the key to any hobby" and metal detecting is no exception. There are simple things you need to do to make the hunting more enjoyable and productive. To get started, here are my favorite tips for you.

Note: If you want to get a metal detector you want to start with, check out those I will be listing later.

The tips for metal detecting are as follow:

- Have the right kit
- Buy the right detector
- Know your local areas
- Avoid trespassing
- Know your detector

In order to get the best results in your metal detector when hunting for a metal make sure that your metal detector is a bit close to the ground so that it will not lose sensitivity. Some people may not place their detector in a good position and that will make their machine to be little difficult to sense the present of metal in the ground. How you place your detector when hunting matters a lot.

Please remember to pay attention to the sound that comes from your metal detector because some signal may not be that audible.

Chapter 2

Learning the Lingo of Metal Detecting

Learning lingo of metal detecting is cool, I will be teaching you some lingo in detecting metal. It might be of help to you before going to hunt your precious metals.

All metals: Most metals have discrimination targets. Detecting without the discrimination signal turned on will allow all the metal objects to result in signal. The discrimination allows you to filter out some junks. All metal mode is usually used in a virgin site where only the valuable metals are likely to be detected.

Bling: It is a fancy jewelry which may be precious metal or may not be precious metal. It is a great thing finding bling. Bling can make you feel surprised at first sight. The best bling is a jewelry that is loaded with valuable metal

Tone ID: This is an audio signal in metal detector which notifies you of the presence of treasures before you can start your digging.

Black dirt: It is naturally enriched common soil in very old site. The present of black dirt can be a sign that you are closer to a treasure.

Visual ID: Technology has gone far. Detector producers have equally built some metal detectors which have small screen that can tell you what is hidden beneath the ground before you can go on with digging.

Black sand: Black sand is a big sign that identifies that you are closer to a gold. They are like iron particles that are so small. They look like sand, but they are not sand. This is desirable at gold-hunting sites, but not at old coin-hunting sites. You have to adjust your metal detector tool because in some cases the metal detector might have a difficult time in working in such place. Some metal detector may not even work at all. It can cause devastation in some metal detectors.

Bucketlister: This is a very special, once in a lifetime find.

Cache: This is coins or jewelry intentionally buried together by someone or group of persons for a long time. They are often buried in a jar, container or vessels. A cache may also be defined as a "cluster" of coins or precious objects found near each other, even if not in the same hole.

Cache hunting: It is specifically searching cluster of coins or precious objects found near each other. It requires different approach to a site than regular metal detecting. If different treasures were buried in places where specific criteria were met – Such as near a place where animal live, near landmarks that could be easily found. Hunting of metal will be easy in such area.

Canslaw: This is a set of aluminum cans left after being hit by a lawnmower. It looks as if someone intentionally scatter those cans. These give a wide variety of signals due to their size variation and can make hunting look difficult in the environment.

Color: This is a term used to describe gold because of its color.

Choppy: It is a sound detector makes when it finds an object that is almost discriminated out. It is often used to describe a questionable signal. Some coins do have choppy signal.

Clad: These are the new coins which have been formulated with mostly non-precious metals. In USA, they are typically silver-colored coins. These coins are usually the sign of modern activity. If they are absent from a hunt, but older coins are present, it's a highly desirable in the location.

Coil: They can be called loop in some countries. It is round wire at the end of a metal detector.

Coilball: It is a part of dirt with a coin inside. They are always great. It is often the last moment of anticipation before discovering the coin's type and age. They are much healthier for you. Sometimes, the edge of the coin is Copper.

Coin spill: This is when a coil spills out of a bag of detectorists without a notice because of the little size of the bag.

Digger: This is a tool used to dig out targets. Also, it is used to describe a person who detects. "Hello, diggers!"

Pennyweight: It is a unit of measurement that is equal to 24 grams.

Friends: They are groups of persons digging good targets in a single hole. The hole was dogged with the help of his friends.

Pinpointer: A small, hand-held metal detector used inside of the open hole/plug to help locate the target.

Assay: Assay is what you can use to identify the purity of treasure whether is a gold, silver or any other metal.

Tot tot: The name might sound weird to you, but it is used to represent playground. It is actually good and fun place to hunt.

Pinpointing: The process of reducing the target to a small area in which to dig, either with the main detecting coil or a hand-held probe. Most metal detectors have a "pinpointing mode" which allows users to audibly construct an "X" on the surface of the ground.

Plug: It is a hole which are carefully dug in the ground so that dirt and grass are not harmed. Digging a good "plug" is the mark of an experience and ethical metal detectorist as it reduces the impact on properties being hunted.

BFO: This stands for Beat Frequency Oscillation. They are older detectors which use the induction balance principle. Often used in very cheap metal detectors and rarely used in coin shooting anymore. Often associated with "old school" detectorists who don't want to give up their machine.

Relic Hunters: A detector enthusiast who searches for common objects and not just precious metals. The searches occur in fields or woods, and often targets reflect early conflicts such as the Civil War in the US.

How to use Your Metal Detector to Hunt

When using your metal detector to hunt in any area of your choice, the way you carry up your metal detector determined whether you will discover treasure or not. Many people do carry their metal detector without positioning them well and they sometimes end up without getting any treasure for the day and someone who is experienced in the hobby will pass the same area and discover treasures. I will teach you how you can use your detector in the field for amazing result.

When you are hunting in the field or any area of your choice with metal detector, please make sure you keep your searchcoil height approximately 1 to 2 inches and your detector must be parallel to the ground for effective results.

Do not work faster or walk like you are in a hurry. Remember you are in the field to search for something important, so you have to be more patient in looking for that. So, you are to walk slowly as you scan your searchcoil in a straight line from side to side while moving your precious coil at a speed of about 2 to 5 feet per second. Make sure you advance the searchcoil about one half the diameter of the searchcoil at the end of each sweep.

Filling Holes

In metal detecting hobby, there is a common task you must fulfill which is filling the hole. So many people make this common mistake during their hunting activities. This behavior of not filling back the hole which you dig during retrieving treasure from underneath is very bad. If you do not fill the hole, the place will look like a war zone and it will cause erosion impact to be felt in that environment. Please do not leave the area you dig without covering the hole properly because it is very necessary.

Destroying of Property

During your hunting time in any land you are given permission to hunt, please be very careful not to destroy any form of property when you are trying to recover treasure. The properties you should avoid their destruction are those like trees, killing animals, destroying plants, and shrubs. You can only remove what you are given permission to remove.

Remove Trash

During your digging to recover treasure, there is 70% sure that you will also dig up trash. It is not a bad thing to see trash. Remember you are digging the ground, so trash encounter is just a normal thing. Once you see trash, bring them out. After your recovery of the treasure you dig earlier, take the trash with you and drop them in a garbage bucket. It will be a very nice thing to do.

Monitor the Environment

Whenever you enter a place to hunt, do not be in a hurry to hunt and go. Try as much as possible to observe the environment well. Example, if you enter a place where there is a gate and the gate is closed when you enter, try and close it when you are leaving. Also, if it was open when you entered, try and leave it open when you are leaving as well. If there is anything you removed when you are digging up your treasure, try and drop them back exactly on the position you met them so that the owner will not be angry with your action.

Chapter 3

What your Detector tells You

Technologists are good because each day they do develop metal detectors that will have additional features. Detectors have been upgraded. They can now provide information that will help you to know exactly what you have found before digging them. If it is something you are interested in and want them out, you can dig them out, and if they are not what you want, you can actually let them be instead of wasting your energy on them. So, in this chapter, I will be teaching you the signs your detector display for your easy comprehension.

Audio Tone

In a metal detector, an audio tone is produced when your detector detects a target. A detected nonferrous target will give a medium –

high tone audio response while a detected ferrous target will give a low tone audio respond. These tones are being produce depending on the type of target/treasure it finds. Make sure you listen carefully to your detector tone.

Target Indicator

In metal detector, targets are referred to as treasures. Target indicator shows which treasure is under the coils.

Target ID Number

This shows the numbers of targets that have been located. This number do have different ranges based on the manufacturer. Some are from –4 to 44 on the X-Terra 305 and –9 to 48 on the X-Terra 505. Negative numbers represent ferrous targets and positive numbers represent

nonferrous targets.

Depth Indicator

The depth indicator is a relative guide to how deep a target is. Depth indicator is based on some machine. They give you how much deep the detector can go. This includes shallow, medium or how deep it can go.

Search Coil

Metal detector search coils are the most vital parts of your detector. Without it, metal detector is of no use. You may be wondering what exactly is search coil. A search coil is the coil of wire at the end of your metal detector used in detecting metals. They often come in different sizes and shapes. Each size offers their own special form of strength and weakness. When the coils are viewed, the small coil is always better than the larger coil when it comes for picking treasures. The 8 inches coil is for all purpose coil which is the most popular coil in metal detecting. The larger coils are always suitable at low mineral ground and where there is not much trash, while a small coil is good in picking treasure where there is much trash. Larger coils are always heavier than lower coil and they can cover much depth. Having more than one coil size is better especially when you face different ground levels, but most detectorists prefer smaller coils.

Know Your Machine

If you really want to go into metal detecting hobby, you really need to know your machine. After you have bought the machine of your choice, the very next thing to do is to spend a quality time and read your manual well. Learn how to operate the detector. You can do some practical in your compound for example buried some gold chain or any metal of your choice and use your metal detector to detect them. That will really help you in knowing how your metal detector works. As year progresses, different companies do bring different kinds of machines. You do not need to be buying different grade of machine each year. Learn how to operate the one you have got. if you master them well, using them to hunt will be enjoyable.

Spending more time mastering and swigging your machine is really a quality time well spent. You can as well build small hunt and buried some different treasure on different spot. They will actually go a long way in helping you master their different tone of operations.

Mineralization

Let us talk about the effect of mineralization and how it affects metal detector during your hunting trips. Mineral is a natural occurring compound. So, almost different parts of the earth actually contain natural materials. There are different kinds of mineral, but we are going to talk about the most occurring one during metal detecting such as nuggets gold. The first mineral is the high mineralization's within the ground whereby the ground is hot on its own and they can contain hot rocks, and another type of mineral is the moderate mineralization whereby there is less mineralization in the ground.

Some of the natural occurring minerals like irons, salt and hematite can affect your metal detector for going deep in the ground to detect a treasure, and also it can affect your detector for not having the ability to discriminate target. Now you have known that the earth contains mineral deposits, you might be rolling with the question in your mind like what metal detector can withstand these minerals?

If you want to detect metal in a mineralized ground, getting a ground balance metal detector is a good choice because the metal detector that have ground balance are best for mineralized ground. Ground balance is a way to collaborate your detector to any environment. Using a ground balance detector, you are telling your detector to ignore earth minerals and find you good metal like gold and others.

Metal Detector Classes

While metal detectors are easy to use, there is also precision electronic instrument. So, understanding the way of the technology basics can go a long way towards knowing how to adjust your detector control from various condition and getting the best from it.

White's Metal Detector

White's metal detector is not just a new detector. You might be hearing the name for the first time. This detector has been in market for a very long time and it has different brands of your choice. This is actually one of my brands of metal detector. This metal detector is much more affordable. As a beginner in metal detecting, you can as well go for this type of metal detector.

They have a good quality, durable and easy to use. I remember vividly in the year 2016 when I purchased this metal detector. I save some cash before I came up with the exact amount to purchase it. I am really happy today that I have such metal detector because it has helped me discovered some coins and other relics.

For some years now, this metal detector has been serving me well and I still have it in my house. The detectors are friendly, and they detect some treasures such as gold, relics, coins, jewelry and so on.

Garret ACE 250 Metal Detector

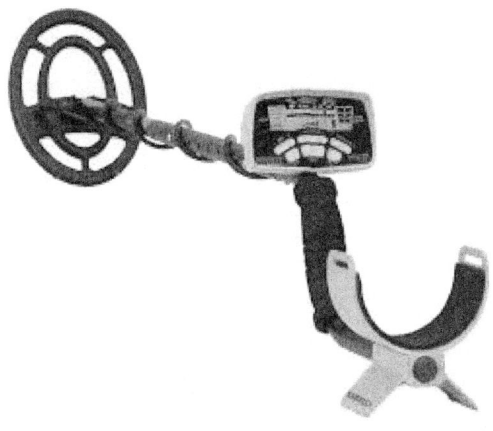

Fig 3: Garrett ACE 250 metal detector

Garrett ACE 250 is the best metal detector for the money. It weighs 2.7bls. So, it is very easy to carry. Garrett ACE 250 has a waterproof property, which means it cannot be damaged by shallow water. It can detect metals such as coins, jewelry, gold, silver, relics and so on .Garrett metal detector works with headphones but it is advisable you get a new one because the one that comes with Garrett ace 250 does not have increased volume. So, get one that has increased volume. The Garrett ACE 250 metal detector has been described regularly as a great beginner's metal detector, durable, lightweight, very simple to use and very affordable. It is a great model to start with when you plan of trying out metal detecting hobby.

Hunting with Your Garrett ACE 250 Metal Detector

When hunting with a metal detector called Garrett ACE 250 and you are a beginner in the field, I will advice you to start your hunting in a sandy area such as playground or beaches. Those areas will make hunting easy for you as a beginner and that will help you to master how your detector works. Garrett ACE 250 is really a good metal detector once you know how to operate it very well.

Can Garrett ACE 250 Find Gold?

Yes, Garrett ACE 250 can find gold. In the other words, all metal detectors can find gold. It all about how deep the gold is and how large it is. The larger the nuggets the easier to detect. The final answer to this question is that, finding gold depends on the ground, The ground can have mineral iron in it, or salt or it can even have the both. The more you get either mineral iron, salt, the harder it is to detect a buried object.

Is a Garrett ACE 250 a Good all Rounder?

Indeed, Garrett 250 metal detector is a good all-rounder and it is really easy to start with it. But remember to be careful when you use it in the beach because only the coil is waterproof while the control panel is not. If you don't plan to throw it in the water, it is good all round.

Teknetics Metal Detector

This metal detector is extremely good as bounty hunter TK4 tracker IV. Teknetics detectors are full of features that allow them to be used in a variety of locations. This detector is owned and operated by the first metal detecting company in the world, Fisher Metal Detector.

It is cool metal detector you can use for treasures in different locations of your choice without any fear. Learning how to operate them is easy. You do not need to spend the whole day looking for who to teach you on how you can operate it. The detector is so simple to learn. It also has a low-price tag. All Teknetics products are set at a reasonable price. You do not have to spend hundreds of dollars to get an upgraded detector, and it is very good for beginners to start with.

Minelab Metal Detector

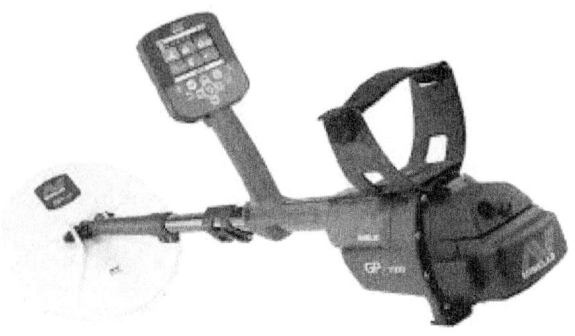

Fig 3.1: Minelab GZP 7000

A minelab metal detector has the feature of detecting gold. This is a gold prospecting model. Gold prospecting model detectors can be expensive. Metal detecting is a fascinating and rewarding activity enjoyed by many people all over the world with an excitement of discovery different treasures such as gold, silver, jewelry and so on.

But in this, we are going to discuss Minelab GPA 7000 because it is the latest gold hunting detector, but they have lesser ones which are good too. GPZ 7000 is very good metal detector in hunting for gold.

It is also a best seller among other metal detectors in the market. The Minelab metal detector can handle almost every environment. It can discriminate between different target (treasure) types and you can set them to reject or ignore unwanted particles (trash).

It is a metal detector for a professional standard in detecting a gold. The GPZ 7000 is the best gold detector on the consumer market. This detector has a higher standard value which you might not found in other metal detectors. It provides extreme sensitivity and depth for gold. The difference between the GPZ 7000 and other detectors is that it is built with zero voltage transmission technology.

This machine can detect gold up to 40% deeper than other detectors as most gold are found in almost in difficult environments with lot of mineralization but the GPZ 7000 makes detecting in such area easy due to its precise automatic detecting ground balance. GPZ 7000 is expensive. But for serious gold hunting, it is best for them. There is also Minelab GPZ 5000 which is cheaper in case if you can't afford GPZ 7000.

Frequently asked Questions

Can Minelab detector detect all kinds of gold?

Yes. Minelab has a range of detector for all gold prospecting levels including professional gold prospecting, small scale artisanal mining, serious holiday gold prospecting, weekend enthusiast and gold specimen collection. It detects all forms of gold.

Can Minelab metal detector tell what a target is likely to be

before I dig it?

Yes. Minelab metal detector has the ability to discriminate between different types of treasures. The discrimination feature on Minelab detector measures two target properties which is ferrous and conductive properties. It detects trash base on their conductive properties.

XP Metal Detector

XP metal detector is one of the biggest manufacturers of metal detectors in the world. The detectors manufactured by this company are lightweight and compactible. They offer exceptional comfort, speed and good performance. The metal detectors are designed perfectly well.

It offers good optimal performance which have quickly become a reference among enthusiasts. It is actually good in exploring dimension fast, deep, light and fully wireless. XP metal detector has Wireless Remote-Control Display Screen, backhead headphone with removable electronic control. There is no wire that may disturb you when hunting. There are so many testimonies about this metal detector from different angles.

Getting one of it is not a bad idea because it detects treasures that many metal detectors might not have the capacity to detect. This metal detector is extremely good for detectorists. As a beginner, it may not be a right choice for you because it is mostly experienced metal hunters that can handle this type of detector. This metal detector can operate well in wet beach, dry beach, relic, gold, coins hunting and so on.

Bounty Hunter TK4 Tracker IV

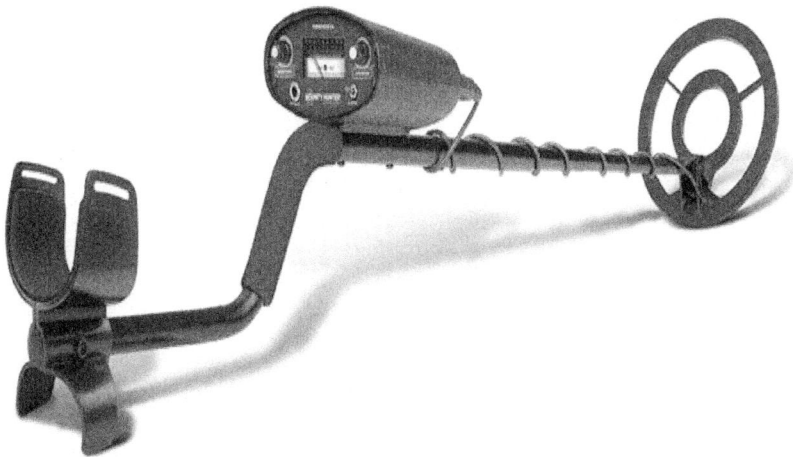

Fig 3.2 Bounty Hunter tk4 Tracker Metal Detector

Bounty Hunter TK4 Tracker IV is a straightforward and affordable metal detector in touch of those looking for basic out of the box of metal detecting functionality. It is also great for children to coach them on how to find treasures hidden in the compound or at the backyard of the house. Bounty hunter TK4 tracker IV metal detector is good for those who have never used metal detector before and want to jump in at a low price point. The tracker is a budget metal detector with a price tag about $130. It might even be lesser than that. It is a simple detector with an analogue display. It comes with sensitive and discrimination adjustment along with a motion of all metal mood and 2 tone audio discrimination. Bounty hunter TK4 tracker IV is a 6.7khz very low frequency (VLF) detector with three modes of operations and it has an adjustable stem. You can easily Adjust it to any size of your choice. They design this product to be rugged so that it can withstand any environment be it tough or smooth. This is a motion metal detector. It must be in motion in order to detect metal.

There is a build in speaker which has ¼ headphone Jack, but I recommend you buy a headphone so that you do not miss a target. Buying headphone jack is going to be a wonderful option so that you will be able to avoid some noise in order for you not to be distract with any form of noise that might be coming from any corner of the environment. Everything about bounty hunter TK4 tracker IV metal detector is streamlined, so it is very easy to use and is also clear. With just two knobs and dual audio tones, it has a quick learning curve, but they can still handle some hurting conditions. The analogue meter shows a signal strength which shows target depth and sizes. The weight of bounty hunter is not that much, it weighs 4.2lbs. It is not the lightest detector, but children can also make use of it because it not much heavy to carry. They can also be used for long hunting. There is no ground balance adjustment function and because of this does not work on ground that contains mineral.

Features and Settings

Fig 3.3: Control panel of bounty hunter TK4 Tracker IV metal detector

Bounty hunter TK4 tracker IV metal detector has three adjustable settings which are sensitivity, search mode and discrimination. We are going to discuss the function of each of the adjustment settings.

Sensitivity

In bounty hunter TK4 Tracker IV metal detector, the sensitivity performs a great work in the hunting of metals. The higher the sensitivity, the deeper the detector will be able to detect a target, while the low the sensitivity, the lesser the capacity of the detector to detect a target. Anyway, there is going to be a problem of a higher sensitivity. The deeper the detector is searching, the more likely to be triggered with the mineralization in the soil. For this reason, you may need to adjust it to a low sensitivity to avoid unwarrant chatter. You can adjust the sensitivity by turning the dial at the left of the control panel

Search mode

Search mode are activated using the switch at the bottom right of the control panel. There are three search modes which are listed below:

1. All metal: All metal mode is used to detect all types of metals such as gold, Silver, aluminum, copper, jewelry. They are also used for relic hunting.

2. Tone: This mode features two tones audio mode with automatic iron rejection. The mode also rejects discrimination settings. It emits on high or low audio signal which depends on the type of metal.

3. Full discrimination: This mode only uses a single tone. Almost all the trash is automatically rejected in this mode. You can adjust the discrimination using discrimination dial.

Discrimination

Discrimination in metal detecting means the ability of metal detector to ignore unwanted target. That is metal that are trash like lead and so on. The bounty hunter TK4 IV has a single knob for discrimination. The higher the setting, the more aggressive the discrimination .But you also need to avoid accidentally discriminating object you want to find because a higher discrimination allows you to find a highly conductive metals without iron signal such as copper and silver. It may reject some important metals like brass, gold.

4. Waterproof search coil: The stock package includes an 8 waterproof search coil, but the control box does not have waterproof so make sure that the control box does not meet water.

Some Usually Ask Questions

Is bounty hunter TK4 Tracker IV metal detector suitable for children?

Yes, it is very suitable for children both teenagers. I personally used it when I was in the teenage level and I enjoyed it because it detects all types of metal. It is much affordable.

Is it suitable for gold hunting?

Like I said before, bounty hunter TK4 tracker IV metal detector can detect all types of metals like gold, silver, copper and all manners of treasures but there is a little problem in gold hunting. The problem is that gold nuggets are often found in a high mineralization area. As the detector lacks automatic ground balance adjustment, it will struggle with a lot of chatter in those area. So, it is not a best choice for gold hunting.

Does it come with warranty?

Yes, it does. The bounty hunter TK4 tracker IV metal detector comes with 5 years warranty.

Chapter 4

Relics Metal Detector

Relics hunting is actually most exciting since there are many different types of relics in the ground waiting to be discovered. Using a quality metal detector is one of the effective ways to find some lost treasures. It is going to be a good luck if you find some relics in your hunting activities. To get relics, you will be needed to be in a place of history and you have to be selective of what relics you are actually looking for so that you can do a lot of research concerning those area before you start your journey of searching. For example, if you want to look in old Spanish history or modern-day hunting from beaches, you need to get good metal detector that will be good in such area. Relics hunting is addictive and fun. You do not necessarily need most expensive detector in the market before hunting for relics. If you are less experienced in metal detecting, I will advice you to go for lesser cost ones so you can work your way into better ones as you proceed. These are some metal detectors that will be good for relics hunting without stress.

They are Garrett AT Pro, minelab CTX 3030, Fisher F22 and so on. If you want to detect relics, you need to go for any of them. They are designed for detecting relics because relics detectors are designed with a low frequency so that they can detect some targets such as iron, brass and others. A lot of relics metal which were discovered always come from mineralized areas. That is why not all metal detectors can detect relics because most metal find it difficult to detect in such environment.

You can use gold metal detector to finds some relics. But not all relics can be found with beach or gold metal detectors because some relics contain irons, steel, brass which most metal detectors always considered as trash. But some of the modern detectors have relics hunting mode which makes all these metals not to be discriminated.

Coins Shooting Metal Detector

One of the most frequent thing people use their metal detectors for is for searching of coins. When searching of coins becomes your hobby, it is known as coins shooting. Coins shooting can be a very good and fantastic way of enjoying your hobby while money is flowing to your pocket. I often say that if you are a good metal detectorist who takes hunting serious and you often go out to look for treasures, you can make a very legitimate cash from all your findings when you sell them. There are several tricks I will be teaching you which will help you in your coins shooting hobby. If coins shooting is your hobby, please adhere to the following instructions:

- If you are interested in coins shooting please try and know coins dealer you can get information from about coins because there are different kinds of coins which you cannot be able to know the value. Tell them and show them any coins you have detect so that they will know how they can buy it from you.
- Please do not scuff the coins or clean them too much after you dig them out because you can destroy valuable coins due to constant cleaning of the surface. It is wise to give any coins you dig out moderate cleaning or leave it in moderate crude state to avoid destroying it. You can clean up silver because they can be in great condition. I recommend you clean up your coins with water that contains little soap. When digging coins, be very careful so that you do not spoil the coins with your digger.

- When you dig up a hole to get coins, please don't be in a hurry to leave because there may be other coins beside the place. So, check well before leaving.
- Using a pinpointer is very cool because many coins are small and can be hard to find in a pile of loose soil. A Pinpointer from Garrett pro is a good option.
- If you are a good coin shooter, discriminate other things accept coins because coin shooting is all about using your time for effective searching. Digging up a lot of trash is time wasting when you know what you are looking for.

So, for good, effective, inexpensive coin shooting, I advise you go for Garrett ACE metal detector. Coin shooting machine also have the ability to discriminate metals like irons.

Underwater Metal Detector

Imagine how fun it will be to be detecting treasure in underwater with a metal detector. Detecting metal in oceans and beaches is a cool one. Technology has gone to the extent that there is metal detector that can withstand deep water. These machines have been powered by electromagnetism. Underwater detector will quickly alert you about the metal object located beneath the water for you to dig regardless of whether you invest pulse induction or very low frequency metal detector. I will give you the list of metal detectors that you can use in water. These are as follow:

- Bounty Hunter Tk4 Tracker underwater metal detector: This detector helps to detect metals under the water.
- Garrett at prounder water metal detector
- Minelab equinox 600 multi IQ underwater metal detector: This detector is fully submersible gadget that provides you with maximum output through minimum effort. This multi frequency machine is able to go about 10ft under the water to find valuable antique pieces that no one has found before whether is a river, stream, lake and so on.
- Kuman automatic underground metal detector
- Kkmoon underwater metal detector which gives you the ability to find the desired valuables at the 30-meter-deep waters. It weighs about 1.2 pounds. It has pulse induction which makes the machine to be suitable for salt and fresh water. Also, it is not a heavy device. So, do not bother about the carriage.
- RM RICOMAX underwater metal detector. This is an underwater metal detector with a longer search coil. It helps to detect deeply buried treasure with a minimum effort.

Gold Metal Detector

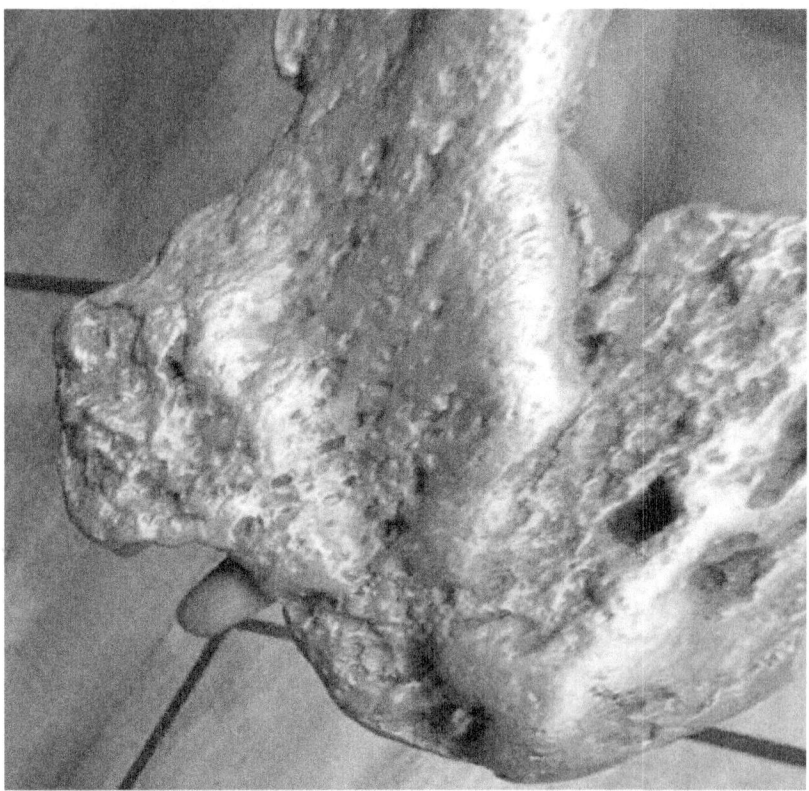

Fig 4: Picture of gold nugget

Metal detector designed for gold is actually an expensive one because not all metal detectors can detect gold nuggets. There are special metal detectors designed for it because if you just pick any metal detector without knowing which treasures it is specialized to detect, you might end up getting no gold at the end of your search. Gold hunting is a lot of fun so do not be discouraged.

So, getting a right metal detector which are specialized in gold is a very good step to take because most gold are found in mineralized area and not all detector can hunt in such environments. I will list some of the metal detectors that are good for hunting gold and they will give you better results in detecting gold both in mineralize and non-mineralized areas. But before we go into that, I will like to give you some factor you must follow before purchasing the detector:

- know your budget because gold detectors can be expensive
- Check if the detector can handle mineralized areas which is an important key because not all detectors can do that
- Before you start your hunting, make sure you make some research on the location. This is an important factor.
- Get a detector with a well manual ground balance
- Choose very low frequency metal detector or pulse induction technology.

These are machines that are good for gold hunting:

- Minelab GPZ 7000
- Minelab GPZ 5000
- Whites goldmaster GMT
- Fisher gold bug 2
- Tesoro lobo superTRAQ
- XP DEUS

Metal Detectors for Kids

Getting a metal detector for your kids is never a bad idea. If your kids actually have interest in metal detecting hobby, please do not stop them. You can help them to achieve their individual goal. My own dad got me a metal detector at my teenage age, and today I am so grateful that he did. At least I now have good practical experience of what metal detecting is all about, and that also increased my knowledge on things I never knew that was existing before. After my hunting I used to do research about my treasure which I got, and I do know several things am not aware of before. Metal detecting is a wonderful hobby for children. It's educational, encourages curiosity, and gets kids to spend more time outside. The hobby is also a great way for adults and children to spend time together.

Metal detecting also helps adults and kids in learning about local history. Choosing metal detector for your kids is not that easy because you do not know which one is the best lightweight design, durable, easy to use, reasonably priced, and you can order it from Amazon for easy and fast supply. The metal detectors for kids are listed below:

1. Bounty Hunter Junior T. I. D
2. Bounty Hunter Tracker IV

3. Fisher F22
4. Garrett ACE 200 and
5. Teknetics Digitek Youth Detector for Teens and Tweens

There are so many others in market. You can make your research and get one for your kids. All these metal detectors I mentioned above have all the properties needed, which are lightweight design, durable, easy to use, and reasonably priced.

Multipurpose Metal Detector

The multipurpose metal detector is a detector which can be used to detect objects in different places without rejecting some important treasures. It can detect gold, silver, coins, relics and so on. In the market, we have metal detector that can perform several tasks at once. That is, it can detect different metals. The first detector I began with was bounty hunter TK4 tracker Iv which is a multipurpose detector and it helped me to discover different kinds of treasures which include coins, jewelry, and it also perform extremely well in beaches.

Multipurpose metal detector is best for beginners because it will detect all types of treasures both for wet and dry land before you can come up with treasures that you are interested in. At your first stage of joining metal detecting hobby, you might have this zeal to detect all treasures. If you fall in this category, then multipurpose metal detector is actually designed for you.

We have several detectors that are good to detect different kinds of treasures. Most of them are Bounty Hunter TK4 Tracker IV Metal Detector, XP Deus Wireless Metal Detector, Garrett ACE 400, Fisher F22 and so many others

Chapter 5

How to Clean Up Your Metal Detector Finds

As a metal detecting hobbyist, I know that you know how rare it is to find something underneath the ground in perfect condition without any dirt or rust. It is close to impossible. There must be dirt in what ever you found buried underground for long period of time. Coins and relics lose their luster each day they are underground. In nature, it is precious metals like gold and silver resist corrosion. But for the most part, iron relics are almost always going to be rusty and pitted.

Brass, bronze, and copper almost always have a patina of some sort. The treasures we find during treasure hunt are to be made clean in order to return to their lost glory. I know that the question that will be running through your mind is, how can I have my finds cleaned? At this stage, I think goggle will be of help to you if you choose to. Checking out in your browser to know how to clean up your treasure which you discovered is a good step to take. But I try my Best to explain some to you.

How to clean Your Found Coins

I will be teaching you the procedures on how you can clean your coins when you found, whether it is silver or copper, or whether is very old or new. The way you clean up your coins really matter. If you clean your coins in a harsh way, it may lose some of its value. So, pay attention to what I am going to teach you now so that all the effort you put in looking for coins will not be a waste.

There are various methods that provide effective cleaning solution without damaging of coins. If you actually want to clean up your coins before selling them, there are appropriate ways to do that but I must warn you never to use jewelry cleaner or metal polish for your coins because those materials can be harsh enough to damage your precious coins and render them useless. Make sure you wash your hands with soap before cleaning up your coins. Before I forget, do not use paper materials to clean up a coin but you can use towel to do that.

Steps to take when Cleaning Up Your Precious Coins

- Opened a tap of water and allow the water to run over your coins. When the water is running on the coins, all the dirt will be knocked away. Fast running water is more effective.
- Soaking your coins in warm soapy water helps to clean up your coins. Just add little detergent inside a bowl of warm water and drop your coins in it. Shake it little by little for effective cleaning, but do not put much coins at once to avoid scratch.
- You can also use a hot running water to Clean up your coins
- You can use toothpick or soft bristled toothbrush to work off any entrusted dirt from your coins
- You can soak your dirty coins in a cup of white vinegar because vinegar contain acid that can remove stubborn dirt from your coins. Please soak the coins for about 40mins for effective cleaning
- A final rinse with distilled water adds shine to your coins and a pat or air dry on a soft towel. Please do not rub your coins. Pat them and allow the sun to do the rest but if the final rinse was with distilled water, just let them air-dry without any patting.

With what I have explained above, I know that you can clean up your coins without any fear. With all these steps, you can remove dirt, grime, germs from your coins and leave them shiny.

Jewelry Cleaning

I will be teaching you the best way to clean jewelry and make it to shine in this section. I will show you how to use around-the-house items for cleaning rings, earrings, necklaces, and more. The best way to clean up your jewelry when you find them and bring it home is to mix a few drops of liquid dish soap with a few cups of water. Then place jewelry in the mixture for a few minutes. After some minutes, you can remove then. Use a clean cloth or soft towel to wipe, dry and buff out any spots. Allow the jewelry to dry before contacting the buyer.

How to Clean Up Your Gold

Gold does not always hold dirt. Anytime you dig out gold, it always shines like it is not dig out from ground. You can easily use a towel to clean it up or the safest way to clean it is to soak the gold in a little warm soapy water, and gently clean it up with a baby brush that do not have sharp edge. After that, dry it with soft cloth or you can airdry it but not under a very hot sun. Please avoid the use of bleach or ammonia to clean gold because those substances are very harsh.

How to clean Iron Relics Using Electrolysis

Electrolysis is what I use in cleaning up my relics because my relics contain stubborn rust in its body. Cleaning of relics can be very hard especially when you do not know a way to go about the cleaning. Imagine an iron that has stayed underground for a long time. The irons must get rust. So, cleaning it to the desire taste will be a little hard but electrolysis have come to play a big role to less the burden for you especially when used correctly.

Electrolysis is great choice to use for relics of potential value. Electrolysis is the process of using a direct electrical current to drive an otherwise non-spontaneous chemical reaction. It is important to use extremely low voltages in short increments. You can buy your electrolysis kit, or you can make your own. Before you start, make sure that you are in a well-ventilated area and nowhere near open flame. One of the by-products of electrolysis is hydrogen gas.

Steps You can Take to clean up lost Relics

- You need power supply and meter
- Pour some water in a plastic bowel and put some kitchen soda inside the plastics bowel

- Connect the (+) to the item you want to sacrifice and attach the minus (-) to the item you want to clean collect the multimeter
- So, put the (+) terminal to the sacrificed item and the min (-) to the object to be cleaned and add them to the bucket
- Power up the electrolysis

Cleaning of the item will take some hours. So, just try and check it regularly until everything goes well. After like 4 hours, the item will be ready. So, you have to turn the power off and bring it out. Use a brush and wash it thoroughly in a bucket of water and rinse it. Your relics are ready to be used at this state.

How to preserve Your Iron Relics

If you want to preserve your iron relics, you are to follow the steps I will teach you in this section. Preserving your relics will make it last longer and look presentable to the buyer, and to do that, make sure that your relics is dried either with oven or sun heat. But oven is faster, so here I will be using oven.

Turn the oven to 200 degrees Celsius, put the iron relics on it, and wait for a minimum of 30 minutes, then bring the relics out. Use a paraffin to conserve your relics and use tea light candles because it is cheap to get, and it is also good conserving material. Make sure you grease the item which you want to preserve very well. When greasing, make sure you did not touch it with your hand because it is usually very hot at that point. Put enough grease when applying it. Allow the paraffin to dry outside the oven and know this in your mind that drying the item in this stage is going to take a little of your time. After your drying, brush the surface very well. At this stage, your relics are preserved.

Rules of Metal Detecting

Every legal activity in this world have rules and regulations. Our school, church, and party ground have rules that are guiding them, and the same thing applies to our individual roads. Without rules and regulations, you will find out that people will start misbehaving in the streets.

In metal detecting hobby, anyone can be part of it, but observing the rules and regulations that is guiding the place you want to hunt is more important than anything. Metal detecting has codes of conduct in England, while in UK I will say is considered one of the most structured and disciplined activity. The use of metal detectors on a scheduled ancient monument requires a license and carries a penalty of imprisonment or fine if not obeyed. So, as a detectorist, you need to contact landowners and get written permission before you can conduct any investigations on their land. They can also agree on how to go about the sharing of whatever you find if the owner is really interested in that.

1. Not trespassing: When searching for treasure, please do not forget to obtain permission from the owner or occupant of the property. Always remember that all lands have owners. Even school, church, parks, and beach have owners. Try and look for the owner whether it is own by private individuals or by public before treasure hunting. Do so in order not to be harassed.
2. Please when detecting for treasures, make sure you avoid places that pipelines was buried or where electric wires might have passed. It is very important so that you will not be expose to danger because some pipelines carrying some flammable liquid or gas can be harmful.
3. Try and stay away from national and state parks or monuments because they are actually off-limits
4. Hunting in a military zone where deep weapon and dangerous equipment may have been buried is highly prohibited
5. Apply reasonable caution in digging toward any target, particularly in areas you are uncertain of the ground conditions because deepseeking detectors can detect concealed pipes, wiring and other potentially dangerous materials. The proper authorities should be notified.

I will personally ask you to seek permission in any land that you know nothing about before you can detect in such areas. Please seek permission from the proper authorities.

Getting Permission for Metal Detecting

Please before you go into metal detecting in private property around old homes, abandoned place, different state, or different countries, try and take permission. In the beginning of this guide, I have listed some of metal detectors that will suit different metal types and I know by now you have got them and also learned how to operate them. Anyway, you can detect metals in an abandoned place near your house. At least, hunting in a close area will grant you permission to know some of the rules and regulations that is guiding the place because there are some places you can hunt treasure without any fear of the owner because the place has been overlooked for so many years. But you have to be careful of any harmful animals. I will advise you to go with someone in that case. Metal detecting in private property around old homes is the fastest way to find rare coins and relics for your collection, but first, you have to get permission from the owner.

Locate the Owner

Locate the owner of the land and inform him/her what you want to detect in his/her private property or farm. If you are given permission to enter and detect your desire treasure, you can go on but if the owner does not want you to detect, then you have no option than to go.

Follow the Rules

In any property you want to detect, if they put any notice on the land that prohibits people from going in there, please try and obey it. That is, if there is a sign that says **keep off**, please there is no reason of going into the property after the owner has made his message clear. Do not bother yourself to hunt in such area.

Asking Face to Face Permission

Try as much as possible to meet the owner of the property face to face because there is higher chance of convincing the owner to agree on your request than when you call or email him or her. Don't be afraid to go to his or her house in order to ask for permission.

Leave Your Gear Somewhere Else

When going to take permission, going with your metal detecting tools is not highly recommended because not everybody knows what metal detector is. Going with your hands empty is more appropriate. You can leave your gear in the car or somewhere else while taking the permission so that the owner will not be afraid when you are coming.

Try and Meet Up Your Agreement with the Owner

Whenever you find a great treasure, try as much as possible to also notify the owner and do not forget to thank him or her before leaving.

Chapter 6

How can You Find Buried Treasure?

I know by now you have successfully purchased your dream metal detector and you are probably filled with excitement to go out and start detecting for treasures. And I also know you understand how the machine works and how to identify the alerts and settings. Furthermore, I know very well that this type of questions will be running through your mind such as, where can I find these treasures (gold, silver, coins, relics, rings and so on)? When I started my hunting hobby, any day I want to go for hunting, this question always crossed my mind. I will teach you some places you can easily find treasures in this chapter.

Where should I start metal detecting?

You can start your metal detecting hunting in these places:

- **local parks:** Old or local parks are better places to look for coins. Coins are always scattered in local parks. You can hunt coins in parks that are close to your house or neighborhood. Those places are always good locations to carry out your metal detecting hunting activities, and it will help you to strengthen your hunting skills because you are likely to see some coins in such old parks that have been abandoned for several years.

  But try to get permission from the authority before you can start hunting there to avoid some misunderstanding .When detecting, make sure you keep your detector parallel to the ground and move slowly for affective detection to take place because the way you position your detector matters when detecting for treasures.

- **Old site:** Old site is all these abandoned houses which their owners might no longer be alive, or they might have moved away from those places because of war or something else. Old site is a prefect place you can easily find treasures but before engaging in any search in such area, you have to make serious research about the place. You can use your local library or search online for historical maps of old homesteads, railroad camps, farms, All these places are good for effective searching of treasures especially if it had never been detected before now.

- **Sidewalk:** A Sidewalk is a good place to start your detecting hobby. Find a sidewalk that people always make use of to begin your search for treasure because sometimes things do fall out and the owners were not be aware of them. With your detector, there is 70% chance that you will find some coins and other treasures which have been buried for a long period of time. So, there is a chance that you can easily find some treasures along a walkway.
- **Beaches**: Beaches are very good places for detecting treasures. I do go to beach to detect some treasures and I can boldly tell you that there is no time I went to beach without having a particular find that will go home with me. Beach hunting is very fun especially when you go there with your friends. If you are living close to a beach, there are higher chances of you detecting everyday. Beach is a place different people come and have fun during swimming and chatting around. There is always a high chance of them losing some of their treasures they come with and because they don't have a detector with them, they couldn't find them. I remember a day a young man was looking for his gold necklace which he bought at expensive price. This young man stayed up to some minutes searching for it. At the end, he was lucky I came over to detect as usual. So,

when he informed me what he was searching for and I decided to help him out, can you imagine that he was even standing on top of the necklace without knowing it. My detector detected it and he was so happy to go home with it. So, you see now that a beach is a good, great place you can detect once you have taken a prior permission from the appropriate authority. Some metal detectors are made to hunt underwater as well, so if yours is, you can also hunt in the shallow waters, increasing your potential of finding targets.

Abandoned buildings: Abandoned building such as abandoned houses, churches, and other old structures are often home to various leftover finds. You have a high chance of detecting some quality treasures because different people lived in such area before. Be sure that you hunt the grounds around the old structures, under and big trees where people may have sought shade in the past, and even inside the structure where you may find hidden treasure under floorboards or in the walls. You may have to do some research to find these types of sites, or you use map to locate such area.

I just listed a few areas you can start your detecting hobby and as time goes on, you can easily come up with other areas to go for metal detecting.

Can You Make Money from Metal Detecting?

In some cases, some people don't expect to get rich with their metal detector. Please don't quit your job because of metal detecting, but you can certainly make some money with a metal detector if you do your research and locate good areas to hunt.

What is the Best Metal Detector in the Market?

This is the question people often ask, "what is the best metal detector in the market today?" But in the real sense, there is no particular answer to that because we have so many metal detectors in the market and all are good detectors and everyday people bring new detector with a new modified function.

If you are looking for how to get a better metal detector, I mean a best metal detector that can match your budget plan, that is good for hunting of relics, gold, silver, jewelry, then this guide book is for you. For over 9 years, I have come across different kinds of metal detectors. I have used some and I have also referred some to my friends and neighbors, and all those metal detectors served them fine. Why not introduce your kids into this hobby called metal detecting, so that they can participate in it during their free periods. Metal detecting for beginners is an exciting discovery.

So, I will be teaching you some of the best metal detectors.

1. **Garrett AT PRO**: This is a best value metal detector which serves in almost all areas of detecting various metals. Garrett AT PRO serve all round in detecting treasures like, gold, silver, relics, and jewelry. So, going for it is never a bad option.
2. **Fisher F22:** This is a cool metal detector. It is suitable for both children and adults. It detects metals all round. As a beginner going for it is never a bad idea. They are easy to carry and easy to operate. That is why your kids can also make use of it.
3. **Minelab Equinox 800**: This metal detector is best for relics hunting, coins, and gold. It can be used on every type of ground. The mode for gold is great for gold nuggets. It is lightweight and can be submersible up to 10 feet. It can withstand any environment. Minelab Equinox 800 has a fast recovery speed and target separation. It is a good metal detector.
4. **Minelab Excalibur II:** If you want to go for metal detecting and scuba diving, then this metal detector is for you. I have a friend who makes use of it and it works perfectly well. This metal detector is waterproof, and it can go deep to 200 feet, but it is more effective on land. It features 17 different frequencies to help you find more coins, relics, jewelry which was buried deep down on the ground. It emits different tones for every frequency that is

the tone for silver will sound different from the tone of relics. It is a best metal detector for fresh water. We also have Garrett ACE 300, Nokta makro simplex, Fisher F75, minelab CTX 3030, whites spectra V3i, GARRETT ATX and so on. Getting any of this detector will be nice.

Metal Detector Accessories

Metal detecting, like every great hobby, is an activity that is made better when you have the right tools. There are many metal detectors in the market which are affordable to choose from. I will list some of the tools that is supposed to be in your metal detector box. These tools are:

1. **Pinpointer**: A pinpoint metal detector is an amazing tool that can be used both for beginners and a very experienced detectorist. It makes detection of treasures easy. Imagine digging a large area to unearth a particular metal. It consumes your time and energy because you don't have a clue knowledge about where the treasure is hidden. When it comes to detecting and digging out treasures from underground, pinpointer plays a major role. As a metal detectorist, there are many tools you need to have and one of the tools is Pinpointer. Pinpointer helps to make your hunting easy. Imagine knowing exactly where the treasure

is located. Is that not cool? Of course, it is very cool. That is the work of Pinpointer. I can remember vividly when I had metal detector without a pinpointer, I really passed through stress during that time because my detector do detect the presence of metal but I found it difficult to get the target until I got one and since then, hunting has been so fun to me to carry out. Getting a Pinpointer for your metal detector is a best choice to take. Pinpointers are similar to detectors but the biggest difference is that the detector has large coils that helps you find the targeted area deep in the ground while Pinpointer will not go deep in the ground, but will find the target less than a centimeter away from the tip of the pinpointer. we have so many Pinpointers in the market. So, get one for yourself on Amazon or somewhere else you can trust.

Let me list some for you. You can go for bounty hunter metal detector, Fisherlab metal detector, minelab metal detector, Teknetics metal detector, XP metal detector, whites electronics metal detector and so on. But, using a Pinpointer, you can easily know where exactly is the treasure before you dig. Waterproof Pinpointer metal detector is the perfect solution when you find yourself in water conditions. The modern underwater Pinpointer metal detector is capable of working to varying depths depending on the model. For example, the Garrett metal detector Pinpointer works to a depth of 10ft. So, nothing will prove to be too problematic.

2. **Battery**: In metal detecting, battery is a great accessory in detecting treasures. Without batteries, your metal detector cannot work. If there is no battery in a detector, it equally means that there is no metal detector. In metal detector, batteries play important role. So, getting extra battery for your detector is a good choice to take so that when your detector battery runs low, you can get them changed.

3. **Headphone**: Almost all metal detectors come with headphones. Headphone is important component of a metal detector because it also helps in savings detector battery. Using speaker makes your detector battery to run down. Using them will help you to discover tiny treasure because you can easily here when your detector beeps than when it is on speaker. You can get one for yourself because the one that comes with many detectors does not have volume regulator.

4. **Digger/Trowel:** In metal detecting, having the right digging tool for the types of ground you are to dig is essential. When choosing the type of tool to go for, choose the one that has lightweight and sharp edge so that it will make your digging simple and less energy consuming.

5. **Metal detecting shovel:** In metal detecting, digging a hole is something you must do and participate in because treasures are always buried underground. So, selecting a

shovel for it will make your digging easy because all grounds are not the same. Shovel is good for relics hunting because relics are always buried deeply in ground. You can use a regular garden shovel or one that is serrated along the edges which was made specifically for detectorists. Remember to fill the hole after your digging.

6. **Metal detector bags:** Metal detector bags are also essential when going for hunt. The bag of metal detector is where you keep all your necessary equipment that you may need for your hunting. Metal detector bag will make all your gear to be in one place and safe.

7. **Pouch**: When detecting for treasures, you need to have something to put all your metal detecting finds in so that they will not get lost. Many detectorists have a favorite pouch that they use for their treasures. You certainly don't want that rare coins you found to fall out of your pocket for the next detectorist to find.

How to recover a Target

- When digging a hole which your metal detector has pinpointed, cut a c-shape to a half circle and dig instead of digging the whole areas. If anything is blocking the passage, remove it with your shovel and dig.

- Retrieve your target from the hole or use a probe to further investigate its location. If you notice that the target is deeper, try and place the excess soil on top of the folded plug.
- Try and replace the loose soil and fold the plug back into the ground. Step on the plug to ensure it will not be pulled up with a lawn mower.

How to research for Treasure

Treasure hunting is all about research. You have to do some research before engaging in treasure hunting. Some treasures such as gold, relics, coins, and silver are hard to find. It is even harder if the treasure hunter does not do proper research. I will be teaching you some procedures you can use to make your research. Research is a systematic investigation over an area and to do this research over a place to hunt. You have to follow these steps:

Identify and develop the place you want to hunt

Before setting up your hunting device in order to go and detect treasure, you have to identify the place you really want to hunt like beach, old historical places, old church building, old site, where war had taken place. You just have to come up with the place your heart goes to carry out your hunting, like during my first start, I did research on the beach before I went there. Taking up a research will make your hunting easy. Coming up with a place you want to hunt is very good and nice step to take.

Do a preliminary search for information in library

To engage in metal detecting hobby, you are to be determined. There is this saying, "determination is the key to success". Metal detecting is not a child's joke. After you have come up with a place you want to go for hunting, the next thing to do is get some books in the library about the place you want to hunt. It is in the book you will have some information regarding the place whether it is going to be conducive for you to hunt for the treasure of your choice or whether it is not going to be conducive to the metal you will like to hunt. Then, you can make a choice whether to go ahead to the place or to change location.

Locate the target

At least by now you have finally come up with the place you can hunt, the next thing to do is to locate the spot you can get a treasure. Some places have maps where all the information about a particular place is written. If you locate your targets, it will help you to detect your dream treasure easily. You can locate your dream treasure through Google Search engine. Also, online browser can provide that for you.

Make a note

When taking up a research, it is important to have a notebook where you can easily jot down some things you have researched on for easy comprehension. Write down everything you learned about the place. Take up the map of the place and make sure that you get a prior permission of the place before you start your hunting.

Chapter 7

Detecting for Treasures in River and Stream

Metal detecting in river and stream is fun. You can discover some coins, jewelry and probably some multiple dropped object like old knives, fishing gear and nautical hardware. If you are a lucky type, you can discover some gold necklaces which might accidentally fell off from the owner, rings which some couples who divorced might angrily pull off and threw into the water and so many valuable things.

Getting a multipurpose metal detector for this job can go a long way in detecting in the river and stream. If you are detecting for only coins and jewelry, then you are to search under bridges and overpasses. Make sure you scan the water and sand very well.

If you are looking for historic relics, you can find places along the river or stream where there is shallow water. You can use a historical book you will get from library or you will buy, and map to know more about the river and stream you are about to detect treasures from. Why for those searching for gold and silver should look for areas in the river where there are outcroppings of gold bearing quartz rock. You can as well search all the places that have rocks, search in the sand thoroughly. There is high chance of seeing a gold.

Note: Please before going to a place to hunt, go with your cell phone and get a toolbox with you.

How to identify Your Metal Detector Finds?

Metal detecting has been a respected hobby for years and I know very well that metal detector is a device you can use to identify different types of treasures like gold, silver, coins and so on but metal detector is not complete if you don't know how to identify your finds accurately. I will be teaching you on how to identify your finds properly.

Technology has gone far because they have come up with a metal detector which can tell you what you detect from the sound it makes. You are going to hear low and high signal. At the LCD of the detector, you will be able to see certain number of bars illuminated on the screen and that is known as target identification indicator (VDI) which tells the kind of metal that is underneath the ground.

How You Can Identify Coins?

Since coins has been the most frequent find in metal detecting hobby, this is a frequent question a detectorist always asks. Where are these coins from? I will teach you some ways you can use to identify coins. Whenever you find coins and you do not have a clear view of the place the coins were first used, take these steps:

- The first thing to do is to search for the coin denomination
- The second thing to do is find the date of the coin and pay attention to the shape
- Identify the size of the coin, the diameter plays a major role in identifying the coin
- Distinguish the coin color
- Try to do research of the image that is on the coin if any. It will help you to make your identification more quickly
- Check the language written on the coin. That will help you to identify what region the coin is from or you can download an app called a coin checker (A coin checker is a coin recognition app. It can identify any coin, including the year and mint, from a photo of the front and back of the coin). This app works perfectly well, and you can get any

other app that suits you to check your coins or try posting photos of your old coin in forums or emailing it to coin dealers. Sooner or later, someone will recognize it in case you find coin that is older to identify.

How to Identify Relics

Relics are from ancient cultures, but some detectorists find it difficult to identify them. Imagine digging out treasure but you do not know what it means. It can be frustrating sometimes. I will teach you how to identify relics. It is difficult to identify exactly the age which the relics have spent or whether it is original or not. The way that you can use to identify your relics is to meet a good archaeologist or museum through forum or other social media platforms.

How to Identify Jewelry

Whenever you find jewelry such as bracelet, ring, brooch, or necklace with your detector, I do not think you will find it difficult to identify because it is something we see each day, but knowing if it is original or fake is the only difficult thing there. To identify original jewelry, you are to search for a hallmark. A single trademark can let you know a great deal about the fineness of the metal, country of origin, a timeframe of manufacture, weight of the piece, or you can get it checked by known jeweler.

How to sell Your Finds?

Metal detecting has gone a long way. Many people derive joy in detecting metal on beaches, local parks, old school, private property with a prior permission and detecting to them have turned to be a hobby. But there is often a big question that one often asks especially when he/she finds a treasure. Where can I sell my finds?

Anyway, so many detectorists do not like to sell what they found because they want it to be a memory to them and they want to show their grandchildren what they discovered at their young age. Also, so many people do sell their own because they want to make some cool money.

Whatever is your own purpose, they are all good. But for those who want to sell their finds, I will be teaching them how to go about that. You can learn from this section.

There are many ways and options that you can use to sell whatever you find during metal detecting.

1. **Shops:** Depending on your country, you can make a research of shops that are close to you that deal on gold or silver if your finds fall in any of the categories. Those

stores that deal on gold or silver will be happy to buy it from you, but it might not be higher price as you expect.

2. **Jewelry selling:** If you find golden jewelry and you want to sell it, going to most of the store that deals on jewelry will make you find the appropriate buyer really fast with a cool price tag. Or you can sell your finds such as jewelry to your family members or friends who show interest of liking the treasure. At least selling it to the people you know will bring more money to you than when you sell it in store.

3. **Relics selling:** If your finds are relics, museum will be a best place to sell them. Once the items are valuable, they will be happy to buy them from you.

4. **Online:** Online selling have been an easy way of selling finds for years. People who always do business online can easily demand for it. If you open e-bay right now and start searching the site, you will find people selling all sorts of things including detected finds. This includes old coins, relic stuff and even gold. eBay has been in existence for years and there are some people who make cool money from it. Anyway, if you intend selling on eBay, they will include some charges such as transportation, but you don't need to panic because the charges will not be much, especially when the items do not have much weight. Also, social media platforms can help you in selling your finds.

Joining a Metal Detecting Club

Fig 7: The picture of a metal detecting club

As a detectorist, if you are searching for mentor that will help you gain more knowledge about metal detecting or you are looking for someone you can share your story with, or proper detecting etiquette about metal detecting hobby, joining a metal detecting club is a good option for you to follow. You have to join metal detecting club because it has a lot of benefits at least for a beginner. As a beginner, there are local clubs you can join such as Michigan Treasure Metal Club or you can browse the one that is closet to your home online and join. If there is no local club close to your area, then consider joining one online. Within a short time, you will see a massive turn out in your metal detecting skill.

Those clubs will help you in so many ways because they give room for questions asking where you can share your thoughts and get all the problems you face during hunting solve. You will see good experienced hunters in metal detecting and also see some beginners like you. If you are using social media platforms, then you can as well join Facebook group clubs such as West Michigan Metal Detecting or Michigan Freedom Diggers. Joining these social media platforms can make communication with your fellow detectorists simple.

Printed in Great Britain
by Amazon